HUNGRY GHOST

Hungry Ghost
Bruce Smith

ISBN: 979-8-9915254-7-3

Library of Congress Control Number: 2025914189

Boston — New York — San Francisco — Baghdad
San Juan — Kyiv — Istanbul — Santiago, Chile
Beijing — Paris — London — Cairo — Madrid
Milan — Melbourne — Jerusalem — Darfur

11 Chestnut St.
Medford, MA 02155

arrowsmithpress@gmail.com
www.arrowsmithpress.com

Cover design by David Wojciechowski at David Wojo Designs

The sixty-eighth Arrowsmith book was typeset & designed by
Gerard Robertson for Askold Melnyczuk & Alex Johnson in Garamond Font

HUNGRY GHOST

Bruce Smith

for Jules

Whenever a thing is done for the first time, it releases a little demon

Emily Dickinson

Previous Books by Bruce Smith

Spill (University of Chicago, 2018)
Devotions (University of Chicago, 2011)
Songs for Two Voices (University of Chicago, 2005)
The Other Lover (University of Chicago, 2000)
Mercy Seat (University of Chicago, 1994)
Silver and Information (University of Georgia, 1985 National Poetry Series)
The Common Wages (Sheep Meadow, 1983)

CONTENTS

ACKNOWLEDGMENTS

The author wishes to thank the editors of the following magazines:

Poetry, American Poetry Review, Agni, Plume, Provincetown Arts, Poem-A-Day/American Academy of Poets, Fogged Clarity, Field, TriQuarterly, Hunger Mountain, Better, Ecotone, New World Writing, Diagram, Sycamore Review, Poetry Congeries, The New Orleans Review, Ampersand, The Times Literary Supplement, The Journal of Applied Poetics, Jung Journal: Culture and Psyche, Forklift, Ohio, Comstock Review, Massachusetts Review, The Progressive Magazine, Blue Earth Review, Juxtaprose, The Nation, Gulf Coast

Dreaming Awake: New Prose Poetry From The US, UK, and Australia, The Golden Shovel Anthology: New Poems Honoring Gwendolyn Brooks

I turned my back on the color fields. I turned my back

on the abstract, New York, the blue/red adjustments

and the inflamed men, the men inflated with trust

and acts of god and gorgeous manly man drag.

I turned my back on the furious magazines [I could

read], their reds and blues and frequencies I used

[I could use] to spin myself into an ecstasy, white

dervish, in custody of a story that begins troubled

with power, then the trouble is you as you spin,

a dance that ends with vertigo, hard light, violence.

In the j'accuse of the US with its expertise,

       its dexterous thumbs, denial, and appetite

for confinement – gated places, meat lockers, love

       of different kinds. I'm ten years into the news

of the death of Eros, born of chaos or beauty, which

       was dominant, which recessive? I'm not sure

I mourned. I'm not sure a soul, self, "I" is what I have

       after or before, which was it? Ten years,

trafficking nerves and cells, I'm not sure I know

violence from preference, the body from the insult.

INCEPTION THICKET

Light wintered over and the names of things

in the emotional body of March, plate tectonics

of the pavement, crust and mantle over and under

thrust in front of the women's shelter, systems

that ramify before, behind the eye, other planetary

March the white black names of things, their real names,

their slave names, something stolen, something seized.

I'm afraid of the matter of fact. What matter? What fact?

Strange attractions and repulsions, cloud discord, black

white facts, corrugated faces, a sheet of paper bitten by rain.

Utopia's sirens annul the contract I had with dream.

The individual wandered off, the assembly adjourned, 4:44 AM

in the ink of it, the body/mind accusing, reminding me of sirens

flexing in the prison yard at noon, to test the system, by the coiled,

electrified voice of Emmett Till's mama, a call to prayer for inmates,

a call to dominion for officers. Night's neck, night's rib

cage, night's wrecked sentence, night's lupine, night's a boy

in a boat in storm wound in his sheet. I'm coming to understand

the asymmetrical nature of art, no target, no trigger, no collateral

damage, no one dies from it, one lives with it like a murmur.

March is a half lie by Heraclitus, mud stuck,

the same becoming, the same global

financial über alles abides. Winter was

an inhuman grammar of the discrete,

heedless hunt and peck, delete.

It was walking on the liquid nitrogen skin

of Saturn. The new boozy atmosphere

scares me with its duende. In it I would be

bourgeoisie, a secretly weeping girl

dressed in her sister's things.

I used a tool to reach a tool I used

to make a tool I used to make

a metaphysics. The crows, those rocket scientists,

those medieval scholars, were exhaustively doing

and knowing the heavy spatial world, writing

their summa, scolding us, singing while dreaming,

knowing foe from friend. I used the body to make

beliefs I used to renounce others I spoke to in words

I thieved from trash and made further rips

in the system and I went on flying with a slice.

THUNDER

When I rubbed myself with my fist and my heart
came into my mouth in that I spat forth the god
of the wind and the air and the goddess of water
                                — Egyptian cosmogony

Summer thunder like sheet metal shaken in a horror movie,

or the ultra, infra sounds turning over in mind: two trains,

one headed North with former slaves, one headed South

with entrepreneurs, one train from the East with a cargo of tear

gas, one from the West with a cargo of tears, arrive at the same

time inside: the wreck of the wreck of their heat speed power

is art and arson, and spit forth the quick evaporated forms

like a man o'war and elusive chords of god and the aftershocks,

oh, the laughter and murder, ha, of the sultry weather

begetter of lies, bugs, begetter of American sobs and water.

I closed the book and changed my life

and changed my life and changed my life

and one more change and I was back here

looking up at a blue sky with russets

and the World was hypnotic, but it wasn't great.

I wanted more range, maybe, more bliss,

I didn't know about bliss. Was bliss just a rant

about the size of the bowl? The trance

was the true thing, no, the rant,

no, the sky, now, that icy whiteness.

To get the syllables correct in the right direction

was to disclose god. The syllables incorrect in

inflection and tone, a glitch in the song, ended wrong

in a line outside the half-way house in the snow

that veiled faces and the world because someone

had pulled the alarm rather than face the shakedown

and melodrama and affliction and unearthed works.

Sirens were the medium for the immediate syntax

of disgrace and me, with my repertoire of words,

a surplus of vowels and my hands over my ears.

The new statues in the Garden of Heroes must be "lifelike or realistic

representations" if deathlike is lifelike, if mute is real, if America,

if Money, Mississippi, if a red wheelbarrow in East Rutherford, NJ.

Life – that protection racket, that fresh peach, that rent, that resilience,

a hospital, Baudelaire said, where patients are possessed with a desire

to switch beds. Realistic the click-bait, the glittering yes, the perpetual party,

the controlled burn, smoke, scratch ticket, tears. Realistic the coma

of cloud space the new statues occupy with eyes that have been sentenced

to life without parole. Their null mouths call for ropes and iconoclasts

to lash them in that way that represents the work of gravity and time.

Season of Death, Season of Skin, Season of No Mellow Fruitfulness,

Season of Fugue, Season of Seizure, Season of Rent, Season

of What Was, Season of Codes, Drops, Pogroms, Season of No Shadow,

Breathless Season, Season of Scat, Season of Hell You Tamboult,

Season Sugared Over, Namesake, Nicknamed, Nameless Season of Death,

Season of All Souls, Season in the Condensery, Tiny Season of My My-ness,

Season of Kitchenette, Season of Whiteness with a Cough, Season

of Figuration, Trickeration, Season of Stalls and Stills, Still..., Season

of Singing Different – Fox Bark and Dialect of Injured Animal, Season

of Can't Go Elsewhere, Can't Meander, Improvise, Season Gone Inside.

It was winter all spring and summer and the streets were inside

us, Season of That Whistling Noise, Season of 1868, De-Skilled

Season, De-Tuned Season Like a Guitar, Season of No Rodeo, I

wore a mask like a bandit, you wore a mask, gown, gloves like

the phantom of the opera, the surgeon of the theater of Us, Season

of Please, Man, Season of Momma, Season of Enumeration, Calibration,

Hum, Season of Please, Man, Season of Someone's Cousin, Someone's

Darker Brother, Season of Spelled Out, Season of the Shipwreck

of The Singular, Flotsam of the Inner Life, Jetsam of Protection Rackets,

Season of the End of The Party, Season of Passing as Someone.

How with this rage …this outrage exchanged like Eros, can't be bought

or sold, but like songs other people play, transferred – hell is songs

other people play – whose instruments are sirens, whose audience

is jurors, whose evidence is spectral: pass it on or tear it up, shall we?

How with this rage shall beauty hold a plea … Beauty in the system, Beauty

busted, cuffed, sentenced, Beauty prosecuted by trauma, Beauty

sang to our wordless verdict, Beauty it curves, mourns, reverbs,

it exposes its throat, Beauty lit by the light of cell phones, Beauty

takes a plea, *How with this rage shall beauty hold a plea whose action is no stronger*

than a flower … one in a bouquet left outside the convenience store.

ROME: PRINCE ROGERS NELSON DEAD

1

I had stage fright before the baroque

    of Rome, afraid some part of me

would get loose in the volutes and the cork-screwed

    columns like the minds of the melancholy

architects that overshot the human. I was dizzy.

        I was thirsty. I didn't know the body

of words. I wanted something burnt or vocal or

    bent around the edges of things like light

when I saw the nuns and polizia point

    above to what? Glory or news

of dread come down in the form of a man

    with a feeling in a truck? Prince, they said,

his voice descending through the grid

    of a speaker in the ceiling of the quick

bar – the song goes on to insert

    seven swords in the virgin mother's heart.

2

How do the architects of beauty

and slavery and paradise and hell,

purveyors of aqueducts and arches,

timelessness, enlargement, things

pressed out of other things

make sense of Prince?

3

Was he Bernini or Borromini in the struggle

of style to break free of god and gravity?

Was he human or un piccolo dio

of celestial helium or the American

demon of hair and skin putting his mouth

all over every fretted thing?

4

Before Babel, before we were confounded in our tongues,

when the whole earth was one language and one speech,

we sang woo, hoo, hoo, hoo /woo, hoo, hoo, hoo,

the nuns to the police, the police

to the besneakered to the flaneurs to the cooks

to the hungry. I didn't know my face.

5

The song weeping from the speaker

glorified and gashed, gilt spilled

in the street, like a church turned inside

out, the glass and pearls crushed

under the heels of Caligula's slipper

are the rhinestones of his cape.

6

Strings lash the inner ear,

like the hero wants to be lashed

to the mast and to hear the sirens

and swoon in the sex of it, but not

succumb, the martyrdom of him

translated, transformed, transfixed –

the skin horripilates like fifteen.

7

American engine and burden, drum

       machine, long synth bass and keyboard –

is it the Revolution or the New Power Generation

       in the key of Catullus? Is the song sentiment

or monument, buzz or blues? A baby coos,

       a rubbery guitar, kick drum on the One and Three.

8

Light bent around the edges of things

       planets, horizons, barrel and tunnel

vaults, windows lavish with ecstatic geometries

       of the ceilings of a mind gyrated

in a *broken waving pediment of flame.*

9

Prince in ruins now, his body a story

       echoed in the two-cycle

engines, the Roman rhythms of triumph

       and defeat, his body wants to be

rocked in a broken waving pediment of flame,

his body demands getting off

the planet not by virtuoso rising up of doves,

but by the spin, the heel toe, the power

and dominion of the cruelly now.

10

Afraid I'd lose myself in perfumes and torques

of the bodies in pleasure and shock,

in the boar's heart, in chords and fugues.

11

When I was Prince Rodgers Nelson

in the USA, I was avatar of Hendrix

and P-Funk All Stars landing the mothership

on the planet, bump transplant, prime

mover in boots doing black as a white boy/

girl and failing, then walking the streets

of Rome leaving a trail of crushed prismatic

beauty, pain, and its cure. Was I straight

or natural hair? Was I Sly, *un buon funky*

or Borromini, groin vault, curled

fretwork, cochlear steeple and wrong to the world?

12

In Prince's erotic city, *world* rhymes with *twirl*,

    spiral columns, volutes, peristyle. Rome

bowed down to lesser emperors, so why not him?

13

I'm not a separatist. The imagination is integrative,

    Ralph Ellison said, *that's how you make the new*

[soul, funk], *by putting something else with what you've got.*

14

The day writhes. He kisses me

    on the mouth because he couldn't kiss

himself. Psyche and Narcissus and Echo.

15

The carabinieri outside the embassy

    hold their Uzis like guitars.

He was born with epilepsy, his people

    were from Louisiana.

Just as you stand before the mixed

use development feeling inner elegy mixed

with ironic outer in a shimmering cultural gloss...

Just as you make a medium that will kill

you, slowly, daily you write it and its line

is a track for the 20th Century Limited, the train

bearing you into the unbearable, how much muchness

can you bear, how much cloud and tremor and fold

and chemical residue and elegy and X?

If grief is love, is love grief?

The dust. The remains. The proof. The groove.

The freight. The ambassador of one or another.

Did it unfold the lie or expose the evening?

Was it a mesh? A mouth? A woo? Whose?

Selectively closed, close, the source, the sex,

murder, a piece of cake. Only connect.

Ping, she said. The noise of the two

machines in vacant ecstasy. I thought

the source a single gush, a synonym,

a single rain, a single hush.

"Cry, Baby" Garnett Mimms & the Enchanters sang & "The Sky is Crying"

sang Elmore James: Two of the songs that stop & frisk sorrow that

take the rent-due, my baby left me & wring the neck of sadness by style. They

are the crying blues [by Mr. Langston Hughes]. They are American. They are

the mouth around a vowel like a dog around a bone. They are quasi

religious. They are quasi profane. Who knows what's the contraband

& what's the lawful crossing into a new territory? The blues because

smuggled pleasure resembles pain, because it enchants, because it is unfinished

From Gwendolyn Brooks, The Womanhood, section I, "the children of the poor":

   "Crying that they are quasi, contraband/because unfinished…"

I dreamed I was speaking to the unmoved, the indifferent, the hostile,

even, wearers of tin foil hats and worse, zealots, believers in belief other

than mine, although how they came to Powell's in Portland, Oregon

to buy my book and read it, I can't understand, some need for blaspheme,

maybe. I had drawn a couple of cross-hatched and blurred lines

that in a certain Northwestern light looked like an insult to everything

dream readers held dear, so that later in the rainy empire outside

cars were overturned and set on fire and embassies were breached

and human beings beaten. No tear gas in the writer, no tear gas in the reader.

The dream is the truth of the lie of the scorn and wish of my tiny my-ness.

HOMERIC

Sang, suffered the singular

Misery limit, holy scheme, fever crisis

Sacked that town, killed the men, seized the women

      as I was seized

Wept, cried, filled with tears

Something brilliant, shining [armor, eyes]

Held a lion, snake, wolf-self, boar, water

Burned thigh bones to the crisis

Sobbed, shed tears, cried, wept, witnessed

Ransacked, hurt, murdered, named by,

      made by, ruined by the song

Thunderstorm like a speech scroll of the Mayans coming from

the south in a language hot as a tear, passive-aggressive enchanted

storm that's sweet as a tea-olive and vicious as history. The smell

is ozone and ethylene and a must of the reconstruction.

The storm unfurls with flint knives and barbs that hack questions

into wet bits of meat, closer the scrolls have feathers or flowers

meaning poetry, that kind of flight or fracture, or an automatic weapon

meaning the local, national, and world news, and closer the hot breath

rolled out of the mouth to your ear are stories of the migrations.

A murmuration of starlings discusses whether they are many or just one.

BEAUTIFUL BOY

1.

After the beautiful boy killed himself I killed myself

and lived in the trash vortex, the j'accuse of the U.S.

with gear and the beclouded night kindness and a mind

like a mule deer in the poorest of zips. My affection

got only so close before I withdrew into self-protection

my white tail an insolent so long. I lived by borrowing

the stillness and dominion and circumference and how dare I

be anything at all, mud under his boot sole, the roux

of the cookbooks he borrowed from the library,

and I returned and wanted stew and the simmering of him.

2.

Where was *the equipment for living?* Where was the witness?

And where was the *Very Rich Hours*: the exchange of rings,

the gathering of flowers? Both *beautiful* and *boy* and April

gone the way of trumpeting May and ghost structures

of the Gothic, costly blue and gold depicting …

Could you say *beautiful* and *boy* after the beautiful boy

killed himself? April felt like retrograde February

impoverished color fields of angry, blowing on our hands

in the Middle Ages of Syracuse where we lived in a university city, joining faith to magical thinking to tactics for fleeing.

3.

After the beautiful boy killed himself *was*

became impossible to hold in one mind, my mind,

and I could not look directly at *is*, the wind

and the thinly branched sapling that is/was his height

and others wore shoes like his shoes with googly eyes,

like was legal and the swellings of April illegal

made up as it was [*was*] of gaps and lapses.

I depended on the vertical hell of other people

for story, for a narrative however broken,

a tolerance that could be that charmed or bitter

could be what takes the place of nouns and verbs.

4.

After the beautiful boy killed himself I was a mackle

of presence, a blurred capital letter that marked

a person's breathing, while he was immaculately

gone except for all the damage to our throats

and to our umbilical selves. Touch was too much

or not enough. White space was obliterated by April's

mute riot or was it organized into caravans stopped …

Ah, what luxury to have his crossed letters on paper,

rationed wartime material we have now in abundance

and map what we know in scratches and around that what?

5.

Cuts, knots, rips, fissures, dots, the ink, drips

from the person after the beautiful boy killed himself,

stop gap concept, the grief counsellor kept it together

or at arm's length so the _____ can't find the _____.

I asked her for experience, and I got a view from above –

grace, I'll take it, the casserole, the pepper pot,

I'll take the fix, the unopened bills for the services

rendered, the renderings billed. Any fix is myopic,

like a mother's look at the child's flaws as virtues

as self-incrimination, the crime being the rich

attachments of subjects, objects, finishes.

6.

Clouds blocked the sun all April

after the beautiful boy killed himself

blocked by the body and the next steps, blocked

the pronouns, blocked *and*, blocked *then*

although, before, so after the beautiful boy

we loved the jagged now for its promise and threat

for its torn map of Detroit and its alternate plans

of duration and what was it yesterday I said

after the beautiful boy killed himself about stopping

me while I was weeping to say go= get out= go on.

7.

What energies and economies of the daily

the obvious snows and obliteration and shoveling

disrupted when the beautiful boy killed himself?

He keeps moving down or is it up? Is there up

in the pedestrian advance to the drug store for more

pain medication, buying a coffee to go and a doughnut?

Why not start from the start from the hesitant

and make a progress that's disrupted by the end,

disrupted by the currency. Are you paying for what

you break or the opposite? How do you intend to pay?

8.

Come back, come back we're asking the highest power

of corporate capital to make you vertical once more

without metaphor – the corporeal you. We will assign the pronoun

by shareholders and trustees who will agree to your exceptional

growth potential, no, growth imperative, to the cult of you

and the evangelism of the ask. We burn, we spread like disease

but the brutal agglomeration of you we love, we pull you up

by your bootstraps, we trade in the sublime machine for you.

We will endure you as you did not endure the terrible world

I thought after the beautiful boy killed himself.

My demon loves the dark money

My demon knows who you are

My demon snapped my spine on the 40-yard line

My demon loves the animal slaughter

By sugar and napalm, by pollen and black sound my demon
        orphaned me

A sparrow crashed against the glass

My demon goes down on you

Then my demon took the world into her body, then seizures.

When my demon says *I*, she means bees, monsters, machines.

It can't be more than 16 x 16, the place where my demon works.

I rose two inches from the subway seat after reading those letters

of yours formed in an order that avoided prisons and perfumes

and scorned the calculus of punishing/consoling while sentencing

the nation to all day and a night by how it treated its nots.

And when I came down, I was wrong to the world and continued

wrong underground wrong in English wrong in Igbo wrong

in the tunnels and wrong on the elevated tracks. To be wrong

was to be half girl, half ardor of the trumpeter. To be wrong

was to be moved by something that was not there, to be seized

by the voice, the ghost, to be vexed and protected by the lovely.

Dickinson in her room writing her wrongness, wrong

to the father brother law and the locomotive of sentences, wrong

to the pronouns, wrong to the gentlewomen and ladies, wrong

to their fabrics – dimity and tulle, wrong to cherubs, wrong

to seraphs, wrong the truth universally acknowledged, it's wrong

to waste paper and the backs of envelopes, and wrong

to love foxgloves – Illuminations – more than humans, wrong

to punish the self and sing off-key and sew the self away, wrong

to fossil them under the bed for sister to burn, so not wrong

to feel death's no end to her and her wrongness.

THE DESCENT FROM THE CROSS

for George Floyd

Is it only for the long white body we can weep – the rib

cage and the throat? A witness holds the viciously long

nails and a witness holds the legs as if they were lumber

in the van der Wyden altar. We are appalled. We are less

than life-size. We become white with unspeakable hurt. What

is the length and heft of someone's son? We are appalled

by the horizontal and we are ashamed of the vertical.

Any cloth we wear is superfluous other than a rag

balled and stuffed in our sockets. We are contorted by

excruciating beauty. We deny we love the manner of his murder.

These are the breaks…Break it up, break it up,

break it up, break down. Breaks in the language, breaks

in the skin, breaks in the angles, breaks in the masculine, the American,

breaks in the [   ], breaks in the now, breaks in the then,

breaks in the phenomenon, breaks in everyone, breaks in the system,

breaks in thee, breaks inside your white history, breaks in the cotton,

breaks in the chain, the pipeline, breaks in my precious

equilibrium when the two-stroke engine begins its complaint,

breaks in the sonnet, breaks in the plot, breaks in the power,

breaks in the watt, *break it up, break it up, break it up, break down.*

*These are the breaks…*Breaks in the song to spin on your head,

breaks in the séance, breaks in the dead, breaks in the bodies of her

and him, breaks in the matter, breaks in the fact, breaks in the air

by the rough-legged hawk, breaks in the *oh, oh, oh* of the hook,

breaks in the fade and the cold ending that breaks me,

thoroughly, finally a break in the murder, break in the need,

breaks in the music in your head – buzz, soul, god – do you hear it?

breaks in the spirit, breaks in the endearing, the disappearing,

the darling, we were alive for the breaking, *break it up,*

break it up, break it up, break down.

after Curtis Blow

Love moved from Eros to Beatrice to virus to Trouble in Mind

to dopamine to money and still they sang, the last romantic men,

the late-century love-me-love-my-hunger-for-beauty men I listened to

like radio for the accounting of angels [earth, baby] and entries

in the book of gin. Friends of the rain, prophets, lovers of the numen,

astonished by fathers and work, dreaming of redeeming. I looked

through the lens of a drop descending a window to see a world reversed

and incandescent: May turned into late November light. None of them

were white, just souls looking to be saved from the nothing their gigantic

magnified eyes saw, vapors and sugars. They sway now like Dutch elms.

Lost the class war, won The Big One, war was our "To Autumn" conspiring to load and bless, to o'er-brim and swell. It was what we made sacrifices for so we could continue to dominate the airwaves and the story boards and fall – Lord, it felt good the sky licking our faces – from grace and occupy space and yell domino. We got to say we. We got to say what the colors were and are and the sizes and who gets to look back at whom and for how long and whistle. We got to say here not there. We got to say who gets to insult beauty and what an event was and how much was enough. Enough was enough, yet we wanted more and still more. We had to make trophies to celebrate our defeat of the dragons and we had to make dragons.

You didn't want the scarlets and the golds, the spectacular season

with its lexicon of light to stand in the way of the work which is

ardor not irony, you had forgot, riding the 88 after holding your paper

transfer for the subway, a ticket to civic tragedy with its frowning

masks or the heat of comedy with its warm, damp weddings

and fire house banquets where the cold meats were served. Money

worked this way as you moved toward it or out from under it –

the biscuit, the bread, you called it, the long green, Vitamin M –

the slang criminal and elliptical, thieving or increasing the currency.

Money's story like mine walking around, dark, hushed, time.

I fell for the marriage plot, the bettering as gender knot, the noose

of caste. *The Communist Manifesto* and *Vanity Fair* were published

in the same year. My plot criminal in its innocence, sadistic in its negligence.

I fell for the murder plot that dumps the bodies somewhere the investigation

must uncover through good poetic legwork and find bits of human

material. The bodies were lovely, it turns out, the skin more than

the grimy fingerprints of the desire machine, surplus from the family

violence. When the swerve comes in the plot, the body jerks

from the volts or the pressure of a palm on the small of the back.

The American plot, push, pull, longing, dread, driving and crying.

You are what the market bears. You are too big to fail.

Shielded from risk, your body loaned to fix that fracture, that

fritz in the system. You are your asks, your occluded debts,

your pay offs for turning it out. You throw good body

after bad. You authorize. You bundle. Your white body

buys a lot of space time. Your body buys a lot of art: marble

and vapor, pixels and culture jams, stamps and silence.

You put your body where your mouth is and commit

to what you can't get and get over. Your body dies a little,

dances a little in the company of other bodies, your economy.

I was white for eight hours, off white for six, ate white,

narcoleptic slept through the din of the 19th century, the 20th,

dreamt I cut that body down, woke up, breathed all the white air

I could, full of guilty sweetness in the rain which darkens everything,

which is another country yet the same country saturated

in gloss and gravity and shadow. I rectified and clarified.

I classified and banked. I remembered then forgot what it was,

a white feeling I could not name, nothing in my mouth

but a pink, bitten tongue, that either kept silent or white

lied. White's paper or heroin or a make-shift grave-marker.

Language, my little boat, punctured from within by Anglo-Saxons

and Romans and Greeks, my mouthful of ocean, my spell for harms

and cures. My bass, alto, soprano vowels, my master's concrete

shoes. Bothered by trade wars and god storms. It is enchained,

enchanted, burdened like music. It is raced and gendered. It walks

into a bar and the bartender says why the alternative to silence?

All my white life it has been grass or winged things, lungs and lips.

It has been the groove and break and the freight. All my white life

it has been currency, memory. I used it for power and for love.

I made screeching sounds to those who would be beseeched.

Every I is a melodramatic I, twitching like an eyelid

in sleep. Aristocrat, temptress, resenter, put upon, puffed

up, sheik. More skeptic now, more legible now through the smoke,

the syllables, now that the sky is hospital blue, cadet gray, more

unseasonable now, and why not ripeness to the core for everybody

in all seasons? Or no seasons with palpable designs on my people

who handed out flyers and washed pots with no language

whose mothers and fathers designed beauty and slavery and forms

of lip-twitching longing. Every you's a dog's body, a sight hound

bred for distance, no depth, no scent, looking for a creature to run down.

Crows warn they can't stop won't stop until they bring the regime

down. This means you and your upright points of pleasure, your law

courts as love language, love language as a way to cuff the victims

and the perps, a way to put a couple of coins in the meter. The ice cream

truck plays racist tunes that make us salivate, vibrates the space

between sweet, cold, and violent. How do we get out of the way

of that music? How do we stop the soft civil war? The air went out

of the air. It was 2020. There was no bliss, only control and the crows

poesia, their outsider art, their racket, and expertise in identifying

and passing on to their offspring who's the enemy and who is not.

THE HOLY LONGING

I will tell you if you promise not to post it. To be alive

is to burn – the body a wick for oxygen and violence

and language. You were begotten of luxury and poverty

and fury you felt when you saw candles, then cultures, then

the planet burning. Of course, it intoxicates, the mix of sex

and salvation and American light which was a theatrical

flame the higher powers sent to unnerve and warm and seduce.

It took prolonged fever to forget the moth-and-flame romance,

the name of the moth and the flame. Who is alive enough to know

this feeling of being an inmate or an honored guest or both?

"ALL MEN SAY 'WHAT' TO ME"

—Emily Dickinson

What to the song as if it were whispered – What

murmur – What mutter – What love – What law – gravity

and larceny – What terror since September when the war

remits the blacksmith's boy on the horrid train father

engineers – What weight the self – What weight the Other –

What stutter – What eclipse – What winged sister –

What scholar – What feral brother – What Republican –

What ghost – What adjustments – What agonies – What

sudden light in the orchards – What frost inside and out –

What Dragon in the Crease – What business – What

resurrection – What readiness – What rat, master, bee.

Something startles me where I thought I was safest

—Whitman

Slow art of night, cheap ovation of day, oceanic traffic, hive buzz,

caterwaul, low moan and high hawk screech. It's trash day in America.

But it's always trash day. Whitman, on the back of the trash truck, wary of glass,

wary of looks from the women and the amorous men with glistening beards.

His America is sweepings and shavings, rind and carcass. He bathes

in the stench of the superflux. A leaking bag of exclamation points

loaded into the hopper with phrenology texts. Part of me

is broken-hearted witness, part of me jury that put him away.

He did time for his noise and buoyancy. Bad knees, bad kidneys —

but the world's cleaner for his labor, a little less venal.

You needed me, Rihanna sings, *ooh you needed*

[6 syllables] *me*, overturning the agon of the blues —

I need you, baby, I need you so bad. She turns around

the I/you like turning a gun into a shovel

into a gun. What's a love song but an unreal gun

with a real outcome? What's a song but a creole of need

and word and nation. Whose nation? Whose word?

Whose translation of Caliban and master? Whose

wicked world? The slurs are snarled articulations

of sex injury and glory. Put a god-sized hole in me.

Love him love his looking out the window at Mrs. White's secured

perimeter and the spectral streets distressed by November where the kids

are shaken down by cops – legs spread, pockets emptied – and hereby

enter the system. Is looking a mandate of heaven or a separate but equal

measure of a nation? My looking reads the occupied territories and

absorbs me in the glorious, shattered window of the bodega.

Smoking on the porch near the wheelchair ramp, she eyes me.

The smoke forms slow cyclones of feeling, love her love her

president, and so begins and ends our civil war, we count

casualties, exchange prisoners, negotiate terms of surrender.

IN IT

1

Are you in the mirror trying on an Anglo name?

Are you in the layer of silver? Are you aligned, broken,

deranged, floating in the vitreous humor? Are you

in the stressed unstressed? In the molecule? In the union?

Are you in the pockets of the heteronormative cargo

shorts? In the cluster of quarter notes? In the time

signatures? Are you in the fire since your birth?

Or in the leisure? In the rhyme of room and storm?

In or out of beauty/truth? Bound, processed, pressured?

Are you in the child's cry, the regress, the wrongness?

2

Are you in the data base? Are you in the distance?

Are you locked or loosed in an adolescence [white, male],

a stranger to the familiar [mute, pale], visited by neorealist

ghosts, by neural blizzards. Are you in the romantic, violent,

heroic, private photos – the fall back baby jump shot finding

nothing but net [ecstatic, melodramatic, frail]? Are you

in the interrupted speech? In the debt ceiling? In demons

[white, netting the ghost baby]? Are you in the loin? The shank?

In the wound? The undone? In the leaves where we've spilled

so much ink? In the ink? In the space [white] you take and take.

3

We had history or not. We had sugar and rot.

We had products and by products and forgot.

We had costs. We had sadomasochistic fruit and reduced

wattage and higher power. We had work and work

at the armory and forgot. Provision we had

and sway. Were we in the amusements or the labor,

the uplift or the down put? We had the subway

and we had the El, the plural pronouns and a person

in the family who did the crime and did the time

and got out and walked through a glass door and bled.

4

Can you make a bird fly out of the hole in my chest?

Can you shoot me [again] in my innocence? You thought

I had a gun when the gun had me and shot me in my

innocence, and shot me in my ease and abundance

and when I spoke shot me and the bullet put a hole

in my wool and in the City of Philadelphia and a hole

in my memory which was the imagination hurt,

a blood clot of time and shot up the body.

I would be inside a woman who would be inside of me

between my eyes, like an acupuncture needle or a luxury.

5

When you ate the slaughtered hog you were in it –

the hammer and the murder and in the boil and skin,

bristle in the feed lot and acorn, in the mud and human

sun and in the ancestral squeal and you went inside

the blood-brain barrier and inside Bruce and the death

of Bruce to the blessed deaths that made the story of I

that was mortified and butterflied by knives

into something of yourself you hungered for

and ate in the fatback and the glorious molecular

messengers and the greasy afterglow and the scrapple.

6

Are you, I ask again, in the body? Are you in the giving away

or the having? Are you in the innermost? In the othering?

When you were in New York were you in Israel or Palestine

or with the Sugar Hill Gang in Jersey? Were you in za'atar, the dialectic sauces, the recto and verso of the sandwich?

Were you in the kept or thrown away: the love seat lugged up

four floors and its cartoon rats. Were you in the second-hand

lexicon of slang and Ovid. Were you in translation, in the dolor

of four o'clock Bronx, in the italicized bus ride? In the rent

that determined fate that determined rain and my dissolving.

7

I see you in the White House. I see you, architects of pain.

I see you in your phosphenes that flash when you release

your fingers from my eye sockets, in documents, in the systems

[security, surveillance, weather], in the naming all the animals

[male], in the staking of claims, in sustained injustice, in

your Etruscan monument, in your Roman armor.

I lived in the lives of others. I occupied that stalled,

exalted space of a book for hours and hours –

in that white oblivion of the margins, in the shiver

and press of the black text, in the outside and in.

HOUSTON, MON AMOUR

Because I loved transport [like Dickinson],

I reloaded my card at disco Krogers

and boarded the 42 which began

in the chicken grease of adolescence

[like a poem] and expressed itself

through 900 arisings and ceasings

of time [I am time, the lizard is time,

the oak is time] that paralleled Alabama

and ended when a woman wiped the city

with *un trozo de seda*, a small piece of silk.

CALLED BACK

Dear Lu, I called and called and you never …

Into which ministry did you go with your Russian

Sable and voodoo? Feeling was tinted by you. Are you

beneath the law but also feverish, afar. Are you at store

for unattainables? In some October you are done

with the compass, the chart. I cannot forgive the world

that kicked you out of Emily Dickinson's house

for laughing at the actress chewing all the scenery.

Maybe you are at the grave where gifts are carried away

by ants and police. You left something. Please call back.

Her herness gone, her pageantry, her Lady Lilith

hair, and I'm X with no mixtape Sentimentia,

no ringing. We had no doctrine of design only

rhyme, only things underlined in red, and codes,

static electricity, *all the sugar, twice the caffeine* of Jolt

Cola. And hunger. You had lavish, reckless language

of eldritch and ichor, you abandoned for the truth.

And the attar of yourself, haute couture, haunts, scarlet

fever, blue smoke. Are you inconsolable but alive

in Irrinois? Here nothing's changed as you liked.

for Lucie Brock-Broido, 1956-2018

Reconsidering how James Brown [nearly] saved America

by first spins then splits, then by lungs then screams

both likenesses of flight and flayed skin, running

from law and lengths of rope into your home, your seething

living room, your museum of forgetting, and what's forgot,

what's fearful could be yelled back as in no place but church,

juke joints, reservations, tent cities, movies, Minneapolis.

He sang what you silenced. He was a wish stitched into

a cape, chord change, new breed, *lost someone* he sings, *please*

and we're Flames behind him trying not to miss a beat.

She loves the work of angiosperms,

how they have inserted themselves in our black-

market, country-music ardors. How

we have inserted ourselves in their elaborate

colonial poking. Their good-cop, bad-cop

interrogations of our apocalyptic ideologies,

she's not so crazy about. Her provisional

resistance is one unrelenting plow woman

bent over squash blossoms [weeping

for the Sioux] fighting the potato bug, Monsanto.

Onondaga rain. Onondaga snow. Driving through

the reservation the radio says: *There's a limit to your love.*

December what. December mort. A minor chord.

A nation. *There's a limit to your care, so carelessly there.*

A song is a drive through, a demon possession, a prison

chaplain. Before I could rent to own, I signed treaties I broke.

I broke a chord. Said I had misgivings, said I was limited

in liability. Snow floats, knows no end to oblivion.

Onondaga nation billboard painted over by someone

hurt by government, what remains is *murder.*

The heritage oaks and black locusts brace for another storm

and the corpse flower and the pomegranate tell the story

of warfare and love. At Kew Gardens a voice says: Live

in the under not overstory. Your story is horizontal. Your culture

equals your height divided by your crimes minus the masculine.

Sediment is sentiment. Your dirt is your demon is your burden

is your alien power. Your strength is your weakness. Boredom is

rage, the way the flower is your blind spot. Be the baobab.

Use lover's language: deranged hungers, luxury you die from.

Be the season, the ice caps melting replicates your face.

Pink in the swamp, spring occupation,

good if you have the orchid inclination,

Dickinson says, good if you want

to root in the ooze of the fetid

ditch dowsed by a god, to divine the pink

flag of the flower, stink and spill,

you in the insurgence of paper, unsecured

borders, the whispering campaign

of wind, newsprint leaks a story:

when snipers get a hit, makes a pink mist.

I walked out with Mrs. Woolf in winter

between tea and dinner to buy a pencil.

It was 1927-2023, waves of *the republican*

army of anonymous trampers had come

and gone: a little person in fawn shoes,

police fingering Uzis at the Iraqi embassy.

The eye rests on beauty, conveniently,

but the inconvenient mind is restless

with the cruel variances and facts

that could be changed [recklessly] by a pencil.

Be a work of art or wear a work of art,

Oscar Wilde said, who was once a cello

in a burnished velvet suit with F holes

and drew across himself a rosined bow

sawing through [plucking] languor and hysteria

[by wit] so the spasms of a life

happened off stage, in rooms and under rooms,

that amorous space realized

in a swoon. The other space the World,

the gaol, the law he was and wore.

Nureyev invented a step, a signature

to his dances: the "double assemblé"

that not even he could dance without

stumbling after two revolutions,

feet at nine-fifteen, turned out completely.

I'm turned out completely at 72

after being 18: multiples of Rimbaud.

Four times defeated by my tactics:

desire to double, desire to turn [out, into],

desire to monster, desire to burn.

The factors, the O, the orchid, the oblivion, the American hungers

as vague as drone targets and enemies, O in shadow, O in ozone,

O in home, O in micro-macro, poetry's Oh – the breath expelled

in private to no one, it changes the nation the way a child's song

changes the nation, it can't slow the fire though a trench is dug,

the word a control line, a backburn, a hot spot of the human,

the secret saved or breeched by the talking cure, the killing cure,

the mouth in an O, an ode to nurses and their slang that alters pain,

ode to the bus driver who sings, O-O-H Child, things are gonna get

easier, as if he couldn't be trusted to speak. To speak is to insult.

STYLES OF IMPRISONMENT

Past selves brawl all night and set off all the alarms

but silently and from inside the body. They recall the paper wasp nest

he destroyed as a boy and the buzzing of the avatars – Babylonian,

savage, possessed. I can see to the bottom of this boy, his vacancy,

his sham solidity: he's water, he's fire, he's virus, he's stung, unforgiving

me. He's you let out in the world to become darling and delinquent

and innocent with a small mouth the size of a needle

you suck all the juice of the realm through. You should be undone

and made to beg. What had wasps done but socialize the beauty?

You will be sentenced to a life of paper and ink and American noise.

Biography

Bruce Smith is the author of seven books of poems, *The Common Wages, Silver and Information, Mercy Seat, The Other Lover, Songs for Two Voices, Devotions,* and *Spill.* He is a recipient of the 2012 William Carlos Williams Award from the Poetry Society of America, and his books have been named as finalists for the National Book Award, the Pulitzer Prize, the National Book Critics Circle Award, and the LA Times Book Award. He lives in Syracuse, NY.

Books by

ARROWSMITH
PRESS

Girls by Oksana Zabuzhko

Bula Matari/Smasher of Rocks by Tom Sleigh

This Carrying Life by Maureen McLane

Cries of Animals Dying by Lawrence Ferlinghetti

Animals in Wartime by Matiop Wal

Divided Mind by George Scialabba

The Jinn by Amira El-Zein

Bergstein
edited by Askold Melnyczuk

Arrow Breaking Apart by Jason Shinder

Beyond Alchemy by Daniel Berrigan

Conscience, Consequence: Reflections on Father Daniel Berrigan
edited by Askold Melnyczuk

Ric's Progress by Donald Hall

Return To The Sea by Etnairis Rivera

The Kingdom of His Will by Catherine Parnell

Eight Notes from the Blue Angel by Marjana Savka

Fifty-Two by Melissa Green

Music In—And On—The Air by Lloyd Schwartz

Magpiety by Melissa Green

Reality Hunger by William Pierce

Soundings: On The Poetry of Melissa Green
edited by Sumita Chakraborty

The Corny Toys by Thomas Sayers Ellis

Black Ops by Martin Edmunds

Museum of Silence by Romeo Oriogun

City of Water by Mitch Manning

Passeggiate by Judith Baumel

Persephone Blues by Oksana Lutsyshyna

The Uncollected Delmore Schwartz
edited by Ben Mazer

The Light Outside by George Kovach

The Blood of San Gennaro by Scott Harney
edited by Megan Marshall

No Sign by Peter Balakian

Firebird by Kythe Heller

In the Hour of War: Poetry From Ukraine
edited by Carolyn Forché and Ilya Kaminsky

A Crash Course in Molotov Cocktails: Poetry of Halyna Kruk
tr. by Amelia Glaser and Yuliya Ilchuk

Don't Close Your Eyes by Hanna Melnyczuk

Tiny Extravaganzas by Diane Mehta

Departures from Rilke by Steven Cramer

On the Road to Lviv by Christopher Merrill
tr. into Ukrainian by Nina Murray

Nothing Bad Has Ever Happened
A Bouquet to Victoria Amelina

The Farewell Light by Nidia Hernández

Downfall of the Straight Line by Charles O. Hartman

The God of Freedom by Yulia Musakovska
tr. Olena Jennings and the author

Away Away by Mark Pawlak

The Miró Worm and the Mysteries of Writing by Sven Birkerts

St. Matthew Passion by Gjertrud Schnackenberg

New and Selected Poems by Glyn Maxwell

A Precise Chaos by Jo-Ann Mort

Coming Ashore by Thomas O'Grady

Where Do You Live? by Jennifer Jean

At the Same Time: New and Selected Poems by Wang Jiaxin

Crimean Fig/ Qirim Inciri by Anastasia Levkova, ed.

The Scent of Man by Tadeusz Dąbrowski

ARROWSMITH is named after the late William Arrowsmith, a renowned classics scholar, literary and film critic. General editor of thirty-three volumes of *The Greek Tragedy in New Translations*, he was also a brilliant translator of Eugenio Montale, Cesare Pavese, and others. Arrowsmith, who taught for years in Boston University's University Professors Program, championed not only the classics and the finest in contemporary literature, he was also passionate about the importance of recognizing the translator's role in bringing the original work to life in a new language.

Like the arrowsmith who turns his arrows straight and true,
a wise person makes his character straight and true.

— Buddha

www.ingramcontent.com/pod-product-compliance
Lightning Source LLC
Chambersburg PA
CBHW041539120626
46551CB00019B/2768